Growing
towards
The Light

A Guide to Encourage Positive Thinking

Growing
towards
The Light

A Guide to Encourage Positive Thinking

Juliet Grainger

Royal Falcon Books

First Edition: March 2005

Reprint 2006

ISBN : 81-7896-043-5

Bahá'í Publishing Trust
F-3/6, Okhla Industrial Area, Phase-I
New Delhi- 110 020, India

Printed at Shri Mangalam Printers, New Delhi

Contents

Preface   ix

- You are Unique   1
- You are a Mine of Hidden Gems   4
- You are Good Enough   6
- Peace   8
- Imagine and Feel Wonder   11
- Love Creates Love   14
- Fear not!   19
- Thoughts and Happiness   23
- Prayer and Meditation   26
- Thanksgiving   30
- Perseverance and Confidence   34
- You are Potentially the Light of the World   37
- Laughter   40
- Value Yourself   43
- Orderliness   46
- Obedience   52
- Turn War into Peace   56
- True Beauty   61
- Presentation Skill   65

- *References*   69
- *Glossary*   72

To
My dear son Joel

Preface

This book is written for children and teenagers. However the material can also be used by adults. Each chapter is self-contained. Each one is all about raising self-esteem. It is designed to be used with a parent or with elders in children's classes, or in groups for discussion.

As a teacher I am very aware of how many children and young people feel negative about themselves. With low self-esteem they are unable to celebrate their own uniqueness. Many also constantly compare themselves to others.

It is my hope that through gaining a better understanding of our purpose for being created we will discover our own individual potential. Life is not about competition, it is about our Personal Best and developing those talents and qualities that are unique to everyone of us. It is about exploring and uncovering these rich gems found within us all.

As a parent these lines have always inspired me: *"Children are the most precious treasure...for in them are the promise and guarantee of the future. They bear the seeds of the character of future society, which is largely shaped by what the adults... do or fail to do with respect to children...An all-embracing love of children, the manner of treating them, the quality of the attention shown to them... are all among the vital aspects of the requisite attitude. Love demands discipline, the courage to accustom children to hardship, not to indulge their whims or leave them entirely to their own devices...."*[*]

---

[*] Riḍván Messeges of the Universal House of Justice, Riḍván 157, 2000, p. 9.

The children should be guided lovingly yet firmly to follow and uphold the moral standards in all situations. *"Every child is potentially the light of the world — and at the same time its darkness; wherefore must the question of education be accounted as of primary importance. From his infancy, the child must be nursed at the breast of God's love, and nurtured in the embrace of His knowledge, that he may radiate light, grow in spirituality, be filled with wisdom and learning, and take on the characteristics of the angelic host..."*[*] I feel that as *"God hath created all humankind in His own image, and after His own likeness,"*[†] therefore not only children but we all must learn to value ourselves.

I would lovingly encourage parents and adults to use this book. The chapters of the book may be studied individually or used for consultation in groups. I have included a number of quotes and affirmations in the chapters and children can learn and repeat them constantly. This would help their spirit and minds to focus on the positive qualities. While studying the book, they can use notebooks to do some of the exercises. There is also a glossary at the end of the book which will help the young readers to understand the words that might be difficult for them.

I hope the book will assist everyone who uses it to value his own self, acquire more positive qualities and develop spiritually realizing that *"man is the highest work of creation, the nearest to God of all creatures."*[††]

* * *

---

[*] Selections from the Writings of 'Abdu'l-Bahá, p. 130, Bahá'í Publishing Trust, Wilmette, Illinois, USA.

[†] Ibid, p. 79.

[††] 'Abdu'l-Bahá, *Paris Talks*, p. 9, Bahá'í Publishing Trust, New Delhi, India.

You are Unique

"O Son of Being!
Thy heart is My home; sanctify it for My
descent. Thy spirit is My place of revelation;
cleanse it for My manifestation."[1]

There is nobody in the world who has been created exactly like you. You are unique. You have your own individual path to follow in life. God has created you with your own talents and capacities which you will discover and develop all through your life. You will soon discover things that you love to do and are good at. When something makes you feel happy and alive inside, it is a good indicator that the thing is worthy of being tried. This could be music, sport or caring for your pets. Life is full of possibilities. There are many different avenues that we can follow. Bahá'u'lláh* tells us that we are like a mine that is rich in gems of inestimable value and that education causes it to reveal its treasures. Our gems come in all different shapes and colours. This is why we cannot compare ourselves to other people because the capacities that they are born with are different from ours. Their destiny will be different because they have different talents and a different personality. The use of the word *inestimable* is significant. It means that

---

* The Founder of the Bahá'í Faith.

we are greater than any value that can be put on us. This is really something that we can think about.

'Abdu'l-Bahá* tells us that the purpose of our lives is to acquire virtues. He tells us that *"Love is the fundamental principle of God's purpose for man..."*[2] and that we have been commanded to love each other as God loves us. Bahá'u'lláh also gives us in the obligatory prayer a very strong reason why God has created us. He writes,

"I bear witness, O my God, that Thou hast created me to know Thee and to worship Thee."[3]

In addition to having a material reason for being created, we have a very important spiritual reason for being here. Here is another quote from Bahá'u'lláh which you can learn:

"Thou art My lamp and My light is in thee."[4]

This is a wonderful quote and reminds us how precious we are. Because we are unique, when we have learnt to value ourselves for what we are, we can then value others for their uniqueness. We can then recognize that our friends and family and all other people are equally important, even when they like completely different things from ourselves. 'Abdu'l-Bahá tells us that a light is beautiful in whatever lamp it shines. It is our differences which, when mixed together, make the world such a special place.

---

* Eldest son of Bahá'u'lláh.

You are Unique

You are a Mine of Hidden Gems

Each one of us is like a different brick that is used to build a house. Each one, whatever the size and shape, is needed to make the house. If one brick is removed, the house is incomplete.

Therefore, we should think that "We are of Great Value to the World!"

'Abdu'l-Bahá says in a prayer that *"Thou art more friend to me than I am to myself."*[5] This means that we should value ourselves and it is good to remember how much we are loved and valued by God. God is always our friend and it is good to remember the above prayer at all times.

You are a Mine of Hidden Gems

"...Regard man as a mine rich in gems of inestimable value. Education can, alone, cause it to reveal its treasures..." [6]

We are all created with many hidden gems within us. As we grow, we begin to develop our individual talents. We all have gifts and abilities which are unique to us. We are quite different even from our brothers and sisters.

All through our lives, as we experience new things and learn through education, we will discover new talents, new gems within us. We can gently draw them out by trying new things and practising them.

Having talents is not about competition. It involves doing the things that make us feel alive. Perhaps we love riding a cycle or bike or swimming, cooking, caring for our pets or writing stories, art or walking, writing poems, or building things. It can be anything.

What do you enjoy? Do you have a notebook? Write down what you like doing. Being kind, loving, compassionate, friendly, brave—all these are talents too. Every day you can add to your list. Your friends and family can help you with ideas. You will begin to see how many things you are good at, and how many things you can do. The more we practise our talents, the more we achieve. The more our gems are polished, the more they gleam and shine. And so will you shine. A fulfilled person is glad to be himself and always gives off a glow.

We never stop discovering new talents in ourselves all our lives.

"In every art and skill God loveth the highest perfection."[7]

Say this until you feel it, and you will know you are good enough just as you are. Remember this line in the *Hidden Words of Bahá'u'lláh:*

"Noble have I created thee, yet thou hast abased thyself. Rise then unto that for which thou wast created."[8]

If we think about this, we will be gentle, kind and loving to ourselves. God created us, and we are all very precious to Him as we are.

You are Good Enough

"the chosen ones of God... should not... content themselves merely with relative distinction and excellence. Rather they should fix their gaze upon nobler heights by setting the counsels and exhortations of the pen of Glory as their supreme goal..." [9]

Athletes have a saying: *your Personal Best is good enough.* Winning is not the most important thing for a good athlete. It is reaching the exellence that is their Personal Best.

It is important to do our best in all that we do, but we must be happy with our own individual best. Life is not a competition about being better than others or the best. There will always be people who are better than us and people who are not so good as us. If we are constantly comparing ourselves we will never be happy. It will also make us dissatisfied with ourselves and envious of others. We are each created as an individual to do our Personal Best and to be content with ourselves as we are.

When you find yourself comparing yourself to others, say quietly to yourself ten times—I am Good Enough! This will remind you that life is not a competition to be better than others. We are here to be ourselves and to learn to be content with our uniqueness.

You are Good Enough

Peace

Here are some more affirmations that will remind you of this:

- I am me.
- I do my best.

We know when we are trying to do our best. It feels good inside. It is to ourselves that we must look. If we try to be like others all the time, we can lose touch with who we are. If we really admire a good quality in another person, we can try and model it in our own life, but in doing this we must choose a role model that will really benefit us. This is why God has always sent us divine educators, so that we can really be shown the right way of living through the example of their lives and teachings. When we put our Personal Best into everything we do, we are engaged in an attempt to fulfil the words of Bahá'u'lláh Who has said: *"In every art and skill God loveth the highest perfection."*[10] We must keep reminding ourselves that we are good enough. God created us the way we are, and we are very precious to Him as we are. When God created us, He did so because He loved us. Each and everyone of us has a unique spiritual purpose, our own path to follow. There is nobody else like us. Therefore, we can aim to set the commandments of God as our goal and strive our best to achieve it.

Peace

"Create in me a pure heart, O my God, and renew a tranquil conscience within me, O my Hope...! Let Thine everlasting melodies breathe tranquillity on me."[11]

In the Bible there is a lovely quote saying, 'Be still and know that I am God'.[*] Then again Jesus tells us: 'Peace I leave with you, my peace I give unto you'.[**] These are wonderful words to absorb and meditate on. When I think of these, I think of still lakes and sparkling sunlit rivers. Can you visualise a beautiful place that makes your heart feel happy and full of calm. We can always take time away from our business just to meditate for a few moments on something beautiful and calming.

Today is all about rushing. We are ruled by the clock. We have to rush to get up, hurry to go to school and to work. As children, we are rushed to the child minder, rushed to school clubs and activities. We rush to do our homework in between. We get so used to tearing around, that when we have a space with nothing to do we rush to fill the time in. Our bodies and minds are still filled with adrenalin. When we have to sit still many of us wriggle and kick our legs. How often do you dash to put the television on, or the computer, or say "I am

---

[*] Psalm 46:10.
[**] John 14:27

bored", even when your rooms are filled with gadgets to entertain and things to do.

We live in a culture of frantic activity and we are attacked continuously with noise and offensive behaviour and mental teasing. We are losing the ability to find quietness and peace within ourselves. This is not good for our health. In between activity, we need rest and stillness for the mind and body to relax.

When we are rushing about, we are unable to use our senses properly. We miss so much and are out of touch with our inner selves. See if you are aware of this rush in yourself? Can you catch yourself when you rush to fill in a space?

Pause, close your eyes and think: *In Thy presence I am still.* Rest in the presence of God. Still your body. Still your mind. Still your hands and feet and relax. Make sure that your face and shoulders are relaxed and that your body is not screwed up with tension. You can give yourself a little shake to loosen up. Remember your breathing. Breathe deeply. Breathe out, breathe in, breathe out, breathe in, breathe out.

When you feel still, you will feel collected and in control. Move slowly, do things in order. Slow your pace, and everything will flow more smoothly. If you are doing a project like drawing or homework lay out what you need before you begin. When you are still from within you will be much more focussed. Before you begin still yourself. Close your eyes for a moment. Feel the presence of God Who is there to help you. Your work will be much better because your mind and thoughts will be focussed and you will be able to draw from the wisdom that is within you. Think these words, they can really help:

In Thy presence I am still.

There is a wonderful hymn that says: "Be still for the presence of the Lord is circling all around". This is so true when we allow ourselves the peace and quietness to feel it. We all need an interval of silence to reflect and to pray. As our bodies need rest our spirits need prayer and meditation to grow. All our happiness and inner strength comes from our inner spiritual selves. We need to remember this part of ourselves and nurture it in order to be whole.

Imagine and Feel Wonder

"...Nature in its essence is the embodiment of My Name, the Maker, the Creator. Its manifestations are diversified by varying causes, and in this diversity there are signs for men of discernment. Nature is God's Will and is its expression in and through the contingent world."[12]

Imagine we were all born blind. Shut your eyes and think what it might feel like. There is a famous lady called Helen Keller who was born in 1880. She was born blind, deaf and dumb. With the help of a wonderful lady called Annie Sullivan, Helen learnt to talk and when she grew up she went to university and lectured all over the world. Life to Helen was an adventure. She travelled, went down a coal mine, was adopted by a tribe of Indians as a blood sister, flew in an open aeroplane and went horse-riding. She did everything she could. She said, "The best and most beautiful things in the world cannot be seen or even touched. They must be felt with the heart."

Most of the time our senses are blind, deaf and dumb. We miss so much around us as we rush around. Life is so busy today that we leave no time to pause with awareness. Try this exercise. Stand still. Close your eyes and listen. What sounds can you hear? Can you hear sounds near you? Can you hear sounds further away?

Perhaps it is a bird call or a train far away, or a dog barking, traffic or voices. It could be the wind in the trees, or the sound of water or the mew of buzzards (birds of prey) above the woods. If you practise this, you will become aware of more and more sounds.

Now open your eyes and look around you, as if you are seeing things for the first time. What can you see? Next time you are outside practise looking. You could study a flower, a tree, a squirrel or a bird. Look at it with fresh eyes. Look at the colour, the shape, the beauty. When you really look at a beautiful thing, you may feel a sense of wonder, joy or excitement inside you. Can you hear birdsong? Can you smell the trees, the grass and the flowers? Nature smells even better after the rain! What are you feeling inside? How are you standing or sitting? What is your body feeling like?

These exercises are like meditation. They connect you to the wonder of being alive. They can make you feel that everything is connected to everything else and you are part of this wholeness. When you feel you are clearly seeing, listening and smelling, try touching the bark of a tree or a shiny fruit or a leaf. It can be anything that you choose. Feel its texture, feel the beauty of it from inside. You can practise this when you look at people. Look at them as if you were seeing them for the first time. Practise thinking 'I like you,' as you look at them. Feel how precious they are, how much you appreciate them. The more you can do this, the more they will feel it and the more they will like you. It's a great way to make friends!

Please try to look with eyes that are new and think about the following quotation given in the Talmud:[*]

"Every blade of grass has its Angel that bends over it and whispers 'Grow, grow.'"

---

[*] The holiest book of the Jews.

Love Creates Love

"O Thou Compassionate God! Bestow upon me a heart which like unto a glass, may be illumined with the light of Thy Love."[13]

One of the first steps we can take for caring about others is to get along with ourselves. This means forgiving ourselves when we make mistakes and liking ourselves, whether we are getting things right or not. When we feel good about ourselves, we will feel good about others too.

It is important not to dwell on our weaknesses but to work steadily towards changing them, bit by bit. As we learn not to judge ourselves harshly, we will gradually learn not to judge others that way.

We cannot hate and love at the same time. What we feel towards some people will be reflected in the way we feel about all people. We are as much part of life as other people; we are all interconnected. In life there is no place for jealousy, hatred and ill will and other negative emotions.

As we begin work on the positive feelings in our friendships and concentrate on our weak points, we will find that other people relate much more positively to us.

Love is caring. Do you show concern for your friends when they are hurt and sad?

Love is to be kind. Are you kind to others?

Love is to be courteous. Do you show courtesy to your family, friends and other people?

Love is to be helpful. Do you help your parents and friends?—help them with jobs, keeping things tidy or do little favours to make them happy?

Love is giving, do you share with your friends and family. Do you make them cards, remember their birthdays? Do you give to the fund, or give to the poor in any way? Do you give toys you have grown out of to others—or clothes? Can you think about some more ways you might give to others?

Love is listening. Do you listen to others when they tell you things? Do you appreciate what they have to say? Good friends are always good listeners.

Love is praising. Do you praise others when they do well, and reassure them when they find something difficult?

When you see your friends and family or meet people who tease you or say unkind things, try thinking *I Like You, I Like You, I Like You.* Say this silently to yourself until you begin to think it. If you feel 'I like you', they will feel your liking. Love starts with liking. We can't love everyone instantly, but we can start with liking them.

When we are feeling good feelings about people, we become warm and radiant. We are reflecting God's gift of love to others. We can become channels of love. Try and learn these quotes.

"O God, make of me a hollow reed from which the pith of self hath been blown, that I may be a

clear channel for Thy Love to reach others."[14]

"So in everything, do to others what you would have them do to you."[*]

The most important thing in experiencing a more worthwhile life is our capacity to love and like people. Love is the greatest force in the world. It is a force that cannot be resisted and it establishes peace, unity and harmony in the world. It is important not to worry and struggle when we don't feel positive feelings, but to gently remould our feelings. We have our whole life to practise.

Affirmations can really help. Try saying some of these to help you until you feel the words inside you.

- I am loving.
- I am very loveable.
- I am liked and I like others.
- I am loved and I love others.

It is a talent to love. The more we fill our heart and mind with loving thoughts, the less space we have for unpleasant thoughts.

- As I love I am loved.
- As I help another I am helped.
- My whole life is filled with a sense of love for people.

---

[*] Matthew 7:12.

Ask God, ask Bahá'u'lláh, ask the Báb or 'Abdu'l-Bahá to make you more loving every day. Express love, show love and you will be loved! The divine power is always there to help you. Pray to love more every day. Ponder on the following quotation. You could try to learn it by heart.

"...we must forget all imaginary causes of difference...that we may associate in perfect love and accord and consider humankind as one family, the surface of the earth as one nationality and all races as one humanity."[15]

Mother Teresa wrote: "My Prayer for you is that you may grow in holiness through love for one another, for where there is Love, there is Peace—and if there is Peace, there is Joy. So keep the joy of loving one another in your hearts, and share this joy with all you meet."

Can you learn this quote from the writings of Bahá'u'lláh?

"Love Me that I may love Thee. If thou lovest Me not, My love can in no wise reach Thee."[16]

God teaches us through all His Messengers that we have been created to love Him, and when we think of Him, we are filled with His love and spirit. Every time we pray we receive His love. You may like to learn this quote:

"All men are God's sheep and God is the tender

shepherd and shows supreme love to His whole flock; nor has He distinguished any above others."[17]

God is in love with all of you and you should live your life radiating that love. Smile, smile and smile. It will lift your heart and that of others. Think:

- God loves me.
- I am very loved.

Think of the song:

> Love is something if you give it away,
> give it away,
> give it away,
> it comes right back to you.

Love Creates Love

Fear not!

Fear not!

" Moving Form of Dust!
I desire communion with thee, but thou wouldst
put no trust in Me.... At all times I am near
unto thee, but thou art ever far from Me..."[18]

In the New Testament there are some beautiful words of Jesus Christ Who said: 'Peace I leave with you; my peace I give unto you; not as the world giveth. Let not your heart be troubled, neither let it be afraid.'[*] When we meditate on these words, we immediately begin to experience a feeling of calm and trust. These spiritual words were meant to reassure us.

Imagine yourself walking beside 'Abdu'l-Bahá, or Bahá'u'lláh, or Jesus or any one of God's divine messengers. Would you be afraid in their presence? All of them told us that when they died and went on to the next world they would be as much with us in spirit as they were when they were physically here. Therefore if we can mentally picture any of them beside us, we will know and feel that we are never alone. We can talk to them and imagine them as our constant companions any time.

Every day when you wake up say to yourself, God is with me. Choose who you feel closest to. In your mind,

---
[*] John 14:27.

go to school with them. If you are worried about anything you can share it with them in your mind. They will give you the right thoughts to help you. You need never feel alone. They are with you always.

I knew a lady called Lizbeth who walked the whole day with Bahá'u'lláh. If she mislaid her glasses, instead of panicking she would ask Bahá'u'lláh to tell her where they were. Then she would carry on doing what she was doing and an image would come to her where to look for her glasses. I always saw her find them. She trusted Bahá'u'lláh for everything. All of her life was God-centred. She radiated joy. As she went about her daily affairs she sang lines of hymns and prayers. Because she was filled with the radiance of the love of God, people sought her uplifting company. She was never lonely. She really knew the power of faith and walked with her hand in Bahá'u'lláh's.

Every afternoon Lizbeth would have a rest because she was in her eighties and got tired. She would lie down in the 'presence of the Lord' as she would call it. Then she would send out healing thoughts to everybody she knew who were ill or unhappy. The expressions she would often use were 'sweeten their souls' and 'turn their darkness into light'. She really was a beacon of light to everyone who knew her. Lizbeth radiated healing thoughts and positivity. Another thing I remember her teaching me was 'how important it was to smile at people in the streets, as this could change somebody's heart or the way they felt for the rest of the day, especially if they were lonely.' Also, she would tell anybody who was sad or heartbroken to smile joyfully at strangers in the street, because by radiating love they would begin to feel better too. You should try this at school and with your friends. She had a great effect on my life. She was a real spiritual example to me.

My son Joel was given a really good song about confidence. You may like to repeat these lines:

Walk tall, walk straight and look the world right in the eye.
That's what my mama told me when I was about knee-high.
She said, "Son be a proud man and hold your head up high;
Walk tall, walk straight and look the world right in the eye."

You try walking in the presence of the Lord with your hand in His. Here is a spiritual quote from the Bible. You may like to learn it to help you feel strong and protected by God. We are assured that He is with us always.

"Trust in the Lord with all thine heart, and lean not unto thine own understading." [19]

Here is a similar one from the Psalms.

"The Lord is my light and my salvation, whom shall I fear? The Lord is the strength of my life, of whom shall I be afraid?" [20]

Live with the thought of God and you will develop a peaceful mind. When I was a child I always loved a quote from *Luke*.

"For, He shall give his angels charge over thee, to keep thee:"[21]

When your mind is filled with thoughts of God, and you actively practise trust, a wonderful feeling develops that you are watched over, protected and guided.

William Wordsworth[*] used to imagine how it would be to talk to Jesus. What would be the look on His face, the tone of His voice? So real did Jesus become to him that he felt that Jesus was his close companion and friend. So, at intervals during the day or evening, you can practise being with Bahá'u'lláh or 'Abdu'l-Bahá or any of God's divine educators. What would They say to you? Imagine the love in Their eyes as They look at you. You are Their beloved child.

'Abdu'l-Bahá says that nothing save that which profiteth us can befall His loved ones.

---

[*]English Romantic poet [1770-1850], whose poems are about simple people and nature.

Thoughts and Happiness

"When a thought of war comes, oppose it by a stronger thought of peace. A thought of hatred must be destroyed by a more powerful thought of love... Thoughts of love are constructive of brotherhood, peace, friendship, and happiness."[22]

Can you see a picture of yourself feeling happy and strong? Making a mental picture is called visualisation. Did you know that people are as happy as they make up their minds to be? You can make a choice. You can choose if you are going to view things in a miserable way or a happy and positive way. Even when something is difficult, we have a choice whether we are going to approach it in a negative or a positive way. There is a saying that *you are what you think.*

We become like we imagine ourselves to be. If we constantly think we are stupid and ugly, we will feel stupid and ugly. If we think of ourselves as radiant and confident, we will feel this way and others will see us like this. It takes practice to be positive, but we must always remember that we were created as noble and worthwhile beings and our life has great purpose. You are uniquely you. There is nobody else the same and nobody else will fulfil what you will create in your life. You have your own path.

Fill your mind with fresh thoughts of faith and hope. Visualise this and pray and it will really become apparent in your life. Commit positive words to memory. Here is a positive one from the Bible to start with. *"The Lord is the strength of my life; of whom shall I be afraid?"*[23] Did you know that people can make themselves ill or well with their thoughts. This is how powerful our thoughts can be.

Put all your problems in God's hands. Pray about it and the right answer will come if we are confident and trusting. Remember how 'Abdu'l-Bahá said over and over again to the people He met—"Are you happy?" He wanted everyone to be happy. He was happy even when He was in prison. He and the others used to tell funny stories in prison to make each other laugh. Even though the conditions were terrible they managed to find happiness. If people can find happiness in terrible circumstances, then we can surely appreciate the favourable conditions in our lives and find happiness with all the good things we have!

When you start practising thanksgiving and appreciate all the wonderful things in your life, you will feel more and more positive. Can you think of ten good things now as you read this? Can you think of another ten things that you can say positively about yourself? Practise this and you will like yourself more every day!

You are a much loved creation of God. Your potential is enormous. You are potentially the light of the world, and your life has great purpose if you have a vision.

Thoughts and Happiness

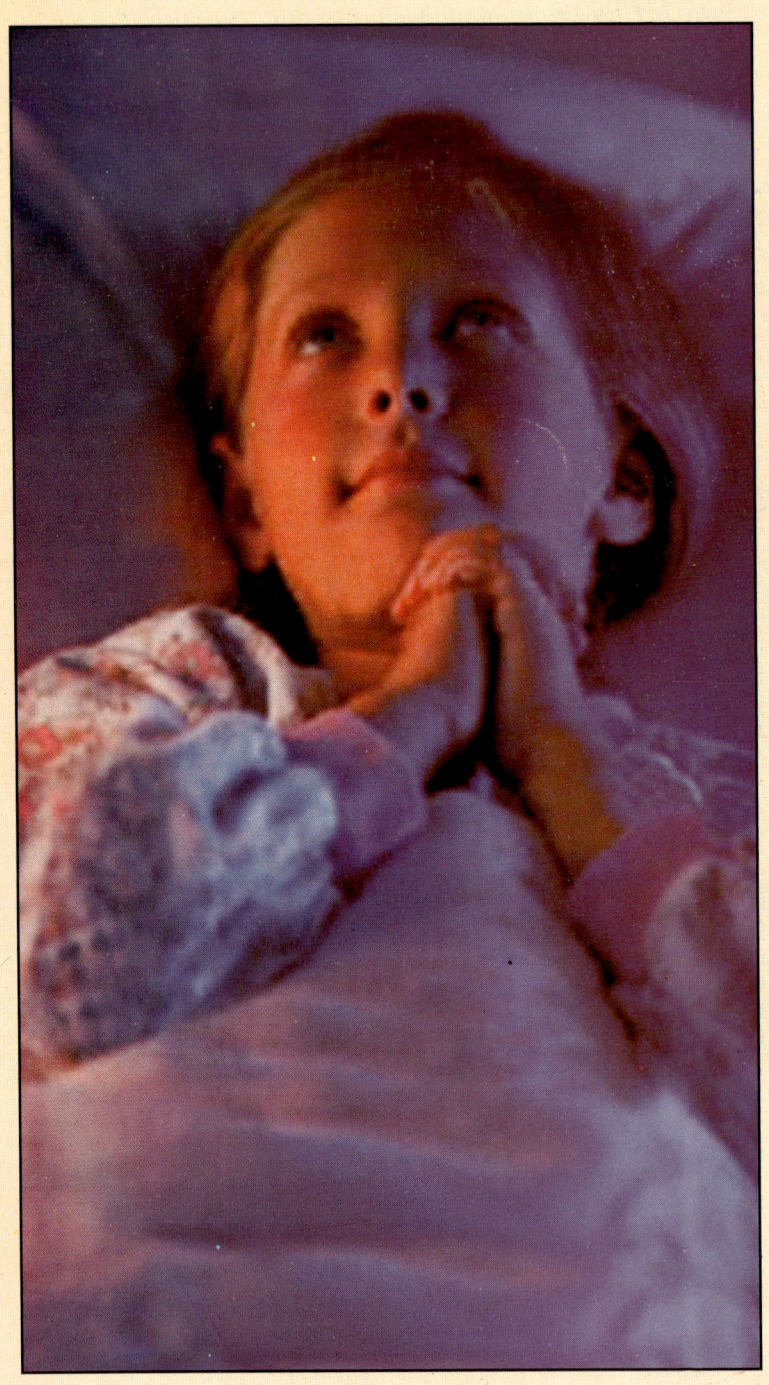

Prayer and Meditation

Can you think and feel these lines about yourself? They will certainly make you feel better.

- I am radiant.
- I am happy.
- I am worthy.
- I am very loveable.

Prayer and Meditation

"Pray to God that He may strengthen you in divine virtue, so that you may be as angels in the world..."[24]

Prayer is conversation with God. When we love someone we want to talk to them and share our thoughts and feelings with them. The more we learn about God's love for us and the more we learn what love means, the more we will wish to spend time in prayer and meditation.

To practise prayer we need to still ourselves, sit quietly and close our eyes if we find this helpful. It helps to practise breathing slowly, by breathing out and then in, slowly. This stops that feeling of rush inside and directs our thoughts to God. Conversation with God is sharing with Him what is in your heart. As with our parents, we can tell Him about things, and ask for help and give Him thanks for all the lovely things happening in our lives. With practice we will come to feel that God is with us and part of us in everything we do. Prayer is also directing our work and art and activities to God. When we create a piece of art, or do a beautiful project at school, or write beautifully or make our beds and help around the house or care for someone who is hurt or tired, we are worshiping God through our work. Work is a form of prayer if it is done in the right spirit to the best of our ability and for the sake of God. This is dedicating something that you are doing to God.

When we pray we have to trust God. Because he loves us so much He knows what is best for us and for our highest good. Prayer may not always be answered in the way that we want it to be, but if we learn to trust in the wisdom of God, we will find out later that it was right for us.

The more we practise prayerfulness, the more we will feel God's presence in our lives. The more we think of God and turn our thoughts to Him, the more we will be aided and assisted. God tells us in all His Holy Books that the more we read His words and think of Him, the more He will be with us. In the *Hidden Words* Bahá'u'lláh says:

"There is no peace for thee save by renouncing thyself and turning unto Me; for it behooveth thee to glory in My name, not in thine own; to put thy trust in Me and not in thyself, since I desire to be loved alone and above all that is." [25]

Prayer gives us hope; it lifts our heart when we feel sad and it gives us answers when we are confused and worried. Prayer is the language of love.

Part of prayer is listening for the answer. To do this, we need to understand what meditation is. Meditation is about making ourselves still and quiet inside so that we can listen to the answers to our prayers. It is a time to empty our mind of all the worries in our lives and centre our thoughts on spiritual things. There are many ways to do this and, when we are older, we can look at the different techniques for meditation. All the religions give ways for meditation. We can contemplate the Writings, or think of beautiful nature or listen to lovely soothing music. It is a time for stillness. It is in quietness that we will hear the answer to our prayers. Our prayers are answered in many ways. It may be in a thought, or in a book that we are reading, or in a dream or in the words that someone speaks to us. After you pray just give thanks to God and trust. The answer will often come in the way we least expect! If we don't allow stillness in our lives, we lose touch with our own spirits and then we will feel sad and empty.

Children who are brought up as Bahá'ís are asked to pray morning and evening by Bahá'u'lláh. Many beautiful prayers have been revealed for this purpose by The Báb, Bahá'u'lláh and 'Abdu'l-Bahá. It is important to say these prayers every day. 'Abdu'l-Bahá explains why we should use the revealed prayers. He says: "We should speak in the language of heaven—in the language of the spirit—for there is a language of the spirit and heart. It is as different from our language as our own language is different from that of the animals, who express themselves only by cries and sounds.

It is the language of the spirit which speaks to God. When, in prayer, we are freed from all outward things and turn to God, then it is as if in our hearts we hear the voice of God. Without words we speak, we communicate, we converse with God and hear the answer... all of us, when we attain to a truly spiritual condition, can sense the Voice of God."*

'Abdu'l-Bahá explains that in order that God may make known His Mind and Will to men, He must speak to them in a language which they can understand. He does this through the words spoken by His messengers. While They are alive They speak to people face to face and convey to them the message of God. After Their death Their message continues to reach men's minds through Their recorded sayings and Writings. This is not the only way in which God can speak with men. There is the 'language of the spirit', which is independent of speech or writing, by which God can commune with and inspire those whose hearts are seeking the truth, wherever they are, and whatever their native race or language. It is by this language that a Messenger of God continues to talk with the faithful after His departure from the material world. Christ continued to converse with, and inspire, His disciples after His crucifixion. In fact, He influenced them more powerfully than before. It is the same with all God's Messengers.

A South African friend of mine called Francesca once said to me: "Learn to breathe prayer as you breathe air." I have always remembered these words.

---

*From a talk of 'Abdu'l-Bahá reported by Miss Ethel J. Rosenburg.

Thanksgiving

"In this day, to thank God for His bounties consisteth in possessing a radiant heart, and a soul open to the promptings of the spirit. This is the essence of thanksgiving."[26]

The best antidote to unhappiness is thanksgiving. We all have times when we feel sad and sorry for ourselves. Perhaps we think some things are unfair. This may be so. 'Abdu'l-Bahá tells us not to dwell on the unpleasant things of life in one of His prayers. He asks us to be happy. If we constantly dwell on the unpleasant things of life and all that is not right in our own personal lives, we will feel miserable; and the more we dwell negatively on the bad things, the more unhappy we will become. We may even become complainers, which is the best way of losing all our friends.

Complainers always dwell on the negative. They cannot see the positive in situations, they never look at what is good but only at what is not. They try and get attention by focusing on what is wrong and then wonder why people avoid their company. They feed their depressed feelings to others and make them feel bad too. Even when good things happen, they will probably miss them because they have trained their minds to think negatively. These people are usually very lonely, but they fail to see why they are so unpopular. Their way of thinking needs to change. We would all hate to be thought of as a complainer!

If we look at all the good things in our life, our hearts will be lifted and we will start to see how good life is and how many things there are to feel grateful about. We will feel happy and excited about life and think ourselves very lucky. It is not the big things that give us a light heart, but the everyday little things. As we learn to feel gratitude and praise, life becomes better and better and we start to see good everywhere. When we think happy thoughts we will have lots of friends. You may also try looking for the funny side of things.

When you get used to the idea of looking for good, you can keep a special notebook. In this you can list all the good things in your life. At first you may only have a few things to list, but as you practise you will think of many more. Here are a few examples that may help you get started.

- I am healthy.
- I am loved.
- I have a lovely home.
- I have a family.
- I have good friends.
- I live with beauty around me.
- I like school.
- I enjoy cubs, brownies, beavers, hobbies.
- I have lovely things.
- I do lots of fun things.
- I eat good food.
- I enjoy TV, computers, games. Write in all your

favorite hobbies and sports.
- I love my pets.
- It's a glorious day.
- I have fulfilling work.
- The world is a beautiful place.
- I have amazing holidays.
- Some things make me laugh.

Your list can go on and on. It will make you aware of all the good things around you. It will confirm how good your life is. Remember to give thanks to God.

There will always be those who are better off than your family. There will always be others who have less than you. The important thing is for us all to learn to be content with what we have. This realisation of what we have can really help us to learn contentment. If we are content, we will be happy and we will feel rich and warm inside.

Be thankful to God for all you have. Be thankful for all His blessings. Be thankful for all your talents.

> *"O God! Refresh and gladden my spirit. Purify my heart. Illumine my powers. I lay all my affairs in Thy hand. Thou art my Guide and my Refuge."*[27]

Any time you are feeling sad this prayer of 'Abdu'l-Bahá may help you.

Every day we can be God-centered and joyous. You may ponder on these words of Bahá'u'lláh and meditate on them?

Thanksgiving

Perseverance and Confidence

"Rejoice with exceeding gladness through My remembrance, for He is indeed with you at all times." [28]

"It behoveth them that are endued with insight and understanding to observe that which will cause joy and radiance." [29]

You may also like to contemplate on the following writings of 'Abdu'l-Bahá:

"Be the source of consolation to every sad one, assist every weak one, be helpful to every indigent one, care for every sick one, be the cause of glorification to every lowly one, and shelter those who are overshadowed by fear." [30]

"May your faces...become so luminous that all your thoughts, words and actions will shine with the spiritual radiance dominating souls." [31]

This will help you to practise positive thinking and to be thankful to Him for His gifts and bestowals.

Perseverance
and Confidence

"...persevere, and face with courage, full faith and confidence such obstacles you can be sure of attaining the goal you have set yourselves to achieve."[32]

One of the most important strengths we can have is perseverance. To keep on firmly doing what we have undertaken. When we take on a project and keep on with it even when it seems hard, we begin to overcome our fear of doing it. When we overcome the difficulty, our confidence and abilities increase.

Everyone of us has something uniquely of our own to offer in this life. It is easy to stifle this potential with fear of failure, low self-esteem and imagined inadequacies. When we make a commitment to complete a task and draw on God for our strength, we will find a way to do it. Maybe we will be guided to the right person to help us, or the right book. If we trust and have confidence, the door will open. Perseverance is not about competition and being the best or the most successful; it is all about doing our Personal Best.

It is really helpful to say a prayer for guidance and help before starting a project or homework. Just sit quietly for a moment, close your eyes and ask God for assistance. Learn to put your trust in Him and you will be amazed at the results. Have you ever done some homework when, instead of feeling boredom, you have suddenly found yourself really interested and excited by the work. You have felt stretched in a really good way. This is what perseverance and using your talents does. Seeking exellence also leads to happiness and liking yourself.

There is a lovely story about a little boy running in a race at his school sports day. He ran as fast as he could, but tripped and fell. He got up and ran on, then tripped again. Then he fell a third time. In an agony of embarrassment and feelings of failure he looked up at his father in the crowd of spectators. He thought he saw his father mouthing to him: "Get up, get up, keep going." And so he did. He got up and ran as fast as he could, even though he was a long way behind all the other runners. He came in last, but everybody cheered him. They cheered far louder for him than for the winners, because they admired him so much for not giving up. This boy had proved himself as a really brave person. What a lot he had to give to life. He was a winner in his own way. I am sure you can think of some instances like this.

Here is an affirmation you can say to yourself:

- With God's help I can handle anything.

You can also try to remember the following quotation at all times.

"Bahá'u'lláh will... bless and crown our efforts with success if we persevere and labour with unabated confidence and vigour." [33]

You are Potentially the Light of the World

"Every child is potentially the light of the world .... From his infancy, the child must be nursed at the breast of God's love, and nurtured in the embrace of His knowledge, that he may radiate light, grow in spirituality, be filled with wisdom and learning..."[34]

'Abdu'l-Bahá tells us that every child is potentially the light of the world. Every child has amazing potential if they are trained from early childhood to develop themselves spiritually, emotionally, physically and mentally. It is for this reason that God has always given mankind laws to live by. He, as our Creator, knows what great potential we have and what greatness we are capable of. A great soul is a noble soul. Sometimes the people who have come from the poorest homes and terrible circumstances can be the wisest, purest and the most noble of human beings.

'Abdu'l-Bahá writes:

"A grain of wheat, when cultivated by the farmer, will yield a whole harvest, and a seed, through the gardener's care will grow into a great tree."[35]

When we feel discouraged and inadequate, this is what we must look at—our great potential.

Here is an exercise that you can do in your exercise book. You may like to do this with a friend, or your parents or a family member or anybody whom you value. Look at yourself and write down all the things you are good at. Write down your qualities too as these are what make you such a worthwhile person. Always remember that when we come to the end of our life in this world and pass on to the next, we don't take our material things with us, or our physical beauty. So it is not our guitars, or skateboards or mathematical skills that go with us, but the talents that we have gained at the personal level through our spiritual development. If we have learnt to serve and love others and used our gifts for the good of our families, friends, people around us and the world, these are the qualities that help to make us the light of the world.

Have confidence in your ability to achieve the best in what you undertake, for if you practise the teachings of Bahá'u'lláh and other inspirational Writings and learn to pray and meditate, you will feel guided and directed spiritually. If we are spiritually happy, it will help us overcome all difficulties while feeling through it all that God is with us and we can experience His love for us in all things. We will learn gradually to breathe God's teachings in our life and they will be part of us in all that we do.

Here is a prayer from 'Abdu'l-Bahá that we can learn:

You are Potentially the Light of the World

Laughter

"O God, guide me, protect me, illumine the lamp of my heart and make me a brilliant star. Thou art the Mighty and the Powerful." [36]

May you beam like a brilliant candle in the world!

Laughter

"My home is the home of peace. My home is the home of joy and delight. My home is the home of laughter and exultation. Whosoever enters through the portals of this home, must go out with gladsome heart. "[37]

Laughter is a wonderful healer. Children have a natural ability to laugh. Laughter is really good for our health and spirit. It relaxes us and it is like a tonic.

Laughter is infectious. When we laugh others catch it and laugh too. As you know, in one of the prayers 'Abdu'l-Bahá says: *"I will no longer be sorrowful and grieved. I will be a happy and joyful being"*. This shows us that we do have a choice. God wants us to be happy and full of laughter and joy. In stories we hear about 'Abdu'l-Bahá, we learn how much laughter there was in his home. He was very good at telling jokes. Laughter made their experiences in the prison bearable. Again and again 'Abdu'l-Bahá told people to be happy. He tells: *"The happiness of man is the fragrance of the love of God."* [38] What a lovely image this gives us of happiness being likened to fragrance. When we smell the scent of a beautiful flower it does heighten our experience.

'Abdu'l-Bahá always asked the friends if they were happy. What would you answer if He had asked you: "Are you happy?"

In some countries there are laughing clubs. Doctors, teachers, people from every profession join these clubs before and after work. There they tell jokes and stories and watch funny films. They laugh real deep belly laughter in the club. They do this because they know that laughter is really good for their health and it strengthens their immune systems. All grown-ups could do this!

Did you know that children laugh on average 150 times a day and adults laugh on average only 6 times a day. During an average day a child smiles 400 times and a grown-up smiles no more than 15 times. Children play an average of 8 hours a day, and an adult plays an average of 20 minutes a day. Children know naturally how to enjoy themselves. What a lot children have to teach adults!

When we laugh out loud, it is like jumping on the spot. It exercises the whole of your body. It stretches and tones all the organs. What a wonderful medicine! When you laugh your muscles are relaxed, the nerves are soothed, your breathing deepens and your circulation is enhanced. Even your blood pressure is stabilised. Also, endorphins which are the body's natural pain-killing chemicals are released. These also help in healing. Medical research has proved that laughter improves the immune system. As children we can teach the grown-ups to laugh. Think how healthy, cheerful and relaxed they would become. Their world would change!

Did you know that people have been cured of terminal illness by laughing. There are stories of very sick people watching comedy films over and over again and listening to and reading funny stories. Laughing brought about physical changes in their bodies and they found themselves completely healed, much to the amazement of their doctors. 'Abdu'l-Bahá says:

"Joy gives us wings! In times of joy our strength is more vital, our intellect keener, and our understanding less clouded. We seem better able to cope with the world and to find our sphere of usefulness." [39]

Let us repeat the following affirmation:

- I am happy and I love to laugh and have fun.

Value Yourself

"God manifested His Love by creating man in His own image. Man must manifest this love by developing himself and others in the image of God."[40]

Everyone of us has been born a perfect creation of God. We are wonderfully designed and made, and it is important that we care for our bodies and minds so that we can fulfil our potential. It is important that we do this wisely.

The media fills our society with ideas through advertising and naturally we wish to fit in with our peer groups in school and around us. This is fine, but we do need to be discriminating in this. We need to be aware of healthy eating and the importance of good food for our general health, appearance and brain function. There is enormous pressure on us from fast food restaurants to take to a diet high in sugar and colourings and flavour enhancers. One look at the increasing popularity of burger restaurants is enough to convince us of this. Unfortunately our bodies get used to all the chips and sauces and it is easy to forget the need to have five portions of fruit and vegetables a day to get the right protecting vitamins and minerals for our long-term health. Bahá'u'lláh wishes us to eat wisely and healthily. It is part of valuing ourselves as a wonderful creation of God. Drinking lots of water and eating lots of fruit and vegetables and fish and meat, organic whenever possible, is really good. We can start by curbing ourselves from always eating fast foods and considering what is best for us.

Self-esteem is all about cherishing ourselves as a beloved creation. The more we value ourselves, the more we will be of value to our society. It is medically proven that a good diet increases our IQ (intelligence quotient) and is beneficial to our mental and emotional well-being. All athletes learn to eat a wise and healthy diet.

Fashion is another area which enormously influences young people. With so much emphasis on sports fashion, it is surprising to see so many slouching, overweight or unhealthy teenagers. Caring for our bodies is another way of valuing ourselves. Taking enough exercise is another way we can change our self-image for the better. When we exercise our bodies sensibly and combine it with the right food, we begin to feel healthy and grounded and carry this healthy awareness of our bodies as we move around. A fit body gives us energy, good skin and a good heart function. Good posture is also very important. Many children learn poor posture and this causes all the internal organs to slump in a wrong position which prevents proper breathing. Children with poor self-esteem tend to slump and lower their heads and avoid eye contact. They feel unworthy and sad. Poor posture also makes us tense up against the cold and hinders healthy blood circulation. The song given in the chapter "Fear not"—*Walk tall, walk straight and look the world right in the eye* is a very good example for us.

Value Yourself

Turn War into Peace

Now consider a car. If we fill it with poor quality fuel, and forget to take it for regular servicing and maintenance, it is going to give us poor service. It will break down and belch out black smoke in the absence of regular oil checks. The brakes will become faulty and it will be a risk to other drivers on the road. Without proper care our body will behave just like this car. Our bodies too need the best fuel, regular maintenance and care. Then it will be a really useful vehicle—a vehicle for our soul. It is therefore very precious and needs to be valued. A useful affirmation could be:

- I like myself, or
- I value myself, or
- I deserve to be cherished.

Can you think of any affirmations for yourself? They must be positive.

Try and walk and sit tall and see the difference it makes to the feeling you have for yourself. Other people will feel your presence much more when you start to value yourself. As you start to feel good about yourself the people around you will sense this and begin to regard you in the same way.

It is good to repeat the affirmation again and again:

- It all starts with yourself.

Orderliness

"Unremitting faith, prayer, the promptings of the soul, Divine assistance—these are among the essentials of progress in any...undertaking. But also of vital importance...is a realistic approach, systematic action. Systematization ensures consistency of lines of action based on well-conceived plans. In a general sense, it implies an orderliness of approach in all ...individual or collective endeavour...it suggests the need to be clear-headed, methodical, efficient, constant, balanced and harmonious."[41]

A beautiful garden is one that has been well tended and organised. If we leave a garden untended and do not weed it and prune back the bushes and shrubs and rake up the leaves, it turns into a wilderness. Very soon the weeds take over and strangle the flowers and brambles and nettles grow over everything.

Our own lives can be like this untended garden. In order to have harmony in our lives we need to bring order into our daily living. This is something we have to work on every day. Orderliness means learning to be tidy. We can learn to keep our rooms tidy, which means finding a place for all our things. After we have played with something, we can get used to returning it to the box or basket or to a certain place in the cupboard or on the shelf, where it belongs. Then next time we want it, we can find it immediately. We need to find a place for our crayons, pens and paper, and all the things we need to write or draw with or to do our homework. Then we can instantly lay our hands on them when they are needed. The same system works with our clean and dirty clothes, our shoes and coats. If we keep them in a fixed place and put them back in the same place, they will always be on hand, and we won't panic and rush around looking for things just before school or going out.

Straightening our beds in the mornings and drawing back our curtains or opening windows is another thing we can do. It only takes a moment, and it is much more pleasant to come home to a fresh and tidy room. Picking up the rubbish and emptying the wastepaper basket is another good habit one can learn. The earlier we learn to do these things, the more organised our lives will become. We will also be much easier to live with. Being neat and clean gives us a good feeling of well-being and contentment. Nobody feels good living in chaos. You will feel out of control when you can't find things and you will probably be a cause of tension to your family and to your teachers. Order in our inward and outward lives brings harmony to our soul. Bahá'u'lláh says,

"Be ye the very essence of cleanliness amongst mankind. This, truly, is what your Lord, the Incomparable, the All-Wise, desireth for you."[42]

When we do our work, we can practise neatness and good presentation. We can learn to set it out well. A teacher will much prefer to look at well presented homework where care has been taken. Care can be seen. It is very different from hastily scribbled work that has been done to get it out of the way. Which kind of work would you prefer?

Imagine what kind of world it would be if surgeons couldn't find their instruments or teachers couldn't find their lesson plans, or bus drivers couldn't find their bus keys, or farmers forgot to set their alarms and milk the cows or feed the animals and mothers forgot to buy the baby milk or to get up to take you to school. Your teachers are at school when you arrive, your mothers and your elders get you to school and the lunch is cooked for you. All these people are there at the right time because they have ordered their lives.

Some people are better at orderliness than others. They will arrive much more peacefully than the ones that rush in at the last minute and who lose things. The younger we are at learning the art of being structured, the easier and more habitual it becomes. It is not automatic, but we all improve with practice. When we are disorganised, we become late for everything.

Being neat and clean in our appearance and hygiene is also part of this orderliness. When we have clean hair and nails and teeth and clean clothes, we will feel much nicer than if we are smelly and unkempt. It shows how much respect we have for ourselves. People with very low self-esteem often become unkempt from discouragement. Others will be immaculate, however hard their circumstances. There is a famous saying: "Cleanliness is next to godliness". All the religions teach mankind to be clean and disciplined. We have to learn self-discipline through practice.

Which garden would you prefer? The one choked with brambles and nettles where there is no room to play, or the one with mown grass for games, and lovely flowers and trees and wildlife? Can you become the gardener of your life?

I have always had great admiration for some of the gypsy[*] families that I have visited when I taught their children. Their caravans were not large, but they were beautifully neat. All the beds were stowed away and everything was shining and clean. The brasses were all sparkling. In order to make room for all the daily living they had to put everything away. You will find this neatness and organisation when people live on boats. There is a wonderful feeling of harmony when you visit these homes. They know how to conserve their energy.

I am going to tell you a true story I wrote for children and adults when I was teaching. I titled the story as 'The Woodland'. It is about a small wood in England that had stood free for fifty years. Unchecked, the trees had grown packed together and the undergrowth had filled in every space between them. Brambles and ivy had spread so tightly that there was little room for birds. Flowers, unable to thrive in the darkness, disappeared from the woodland floor, where once bluebells and wood anemones had carpeted the ground with blue and white. Even the wild garlic had given up the battle. In spite of its wildness the woodland was strangely devoid of

---

[*] People scattered across Europe and North America moving from place to place to find pasture and food.

birdsong and few wild animals made their home in its strangled, gloomy interior. It was as if a silent apathy had spread over all, slowly smothering the life force. Not even the scream of a vixen (a female fox) or the screech of an owl could be heard at night.

It was to this wood that Col came one summer morning. He drove an old Landrover, which towed an equally antiquated caravan. He had arrived to make the wood his home for the next few months. He worked for the 'Royal Society for the Protection of Birds'. They had recently been donated the wood and as a warden for the area it was his job to clean up the wood and to make it once again suitable for birds and wildlife. They had seen that it was a wood that was in such disorder that it was choking and destroying itself through neglect. Col had organised a group of volunteers to help him. In no time, they all began clearing away undergrowth and brambles under his direction. They cut down the rotten trees, leaving the trunks for the insects and wildlife to make their homes. Gradually, glades (openings) appeared where the sunlight could filter through. Nest boxes for owls, woodpeckers, small birds and bats were put up.

All winter Col and his team worked. The wood under its new discipline and care became transformed. Gradually birds were returning and by March early mornings produced a wonderful dawn chorus. It was as if some silent messenger had whispered on the wind to all the birds and animals in the vicinity that the wood had been recreated and had come alive. Badgers, roe deer, foxes and many species of birds had returned.

Seeds from their droppings seeded themselves, and the wind carried plants to the sun-filled glades. The bluebells and primroses once again pushed up without the brambles to choke them. The birds were again nesting and new saplings were pushing up in the spaces. With the pruning and cutting back the light had been let in, and the darkness caused by choking vegetation dispelled. In just a few months Col and his team had brought the wood back in check, and with it he had laid the foundation for life, light and growth. A useless wood had been transformed once more into a thriving habitat.

This is my example of how order has transformed a wood. Perhaps we can now think about ways in which we can release some things in our lives, and tidy up to give space for better things and to allow more light into our lives.

What can I release to let more light and order into my life? Have a think about it.

Obedience

"The source of all good is trust in God, submission unto His command, and contentment with His holy will and pleasure." [43]

In recent times, children are taught to express themselves and make decisions. It is commendable to learn decision making and become confident, but it is easy to forget the role of parents in our life. Most of us have excellent parents who really care for their children. However, as children, once we start school, it is very easy for us to forget all that they have done for us and sacrificed for us. We don't remember all those nights they remained awake when we were ill and the evenings out and social life they have sacrificed for the sake of being with us. Then there are the bedtime stories and the millions of things they have done for us. They have done all this out of their love for us.

The Holy Books* have also asked us to love and respect our parents. If we learn to respect our parents' wishes, we are learning obedience to the will of God. So often we despise their rules that are mostly for our own good. A parent can see when we are over-tired, much better than we ourselves can. They can see how tired we will be for school the next day, so they ask us

---

* Bhagvad Gita, Qur'án, Bible are the Holy Books.

to go to bed on time. To most children this will seem unfair, especially if our friends go to bed later, but we need to respect the wishes of our parents as they desire our welfare. Bahá'u'lláh says:

> *"Beware lest ye commit that which would sadden the hearts of your fathers and mothers. Follow ye the path of Truth which indeed is a straight path. Should anyone give you a choice between the opportunity to render a service to Me and a service to them, choose ye to serve them, and let such service be a path leading you to Me".*[44]

Obedience is accepting a just authority such as our parents and our teachers. The purpose of obedience is to guide and protect us. Rules are made to protect and help us. If we all made up our own rules life would become chaotic. If we decided to drive over traffic lights on red, or disobey the speed limit, or cross railway crossings when the red light was flashing, there would be many deaths and terrible accidents. Parents and teachers make rules for our own safety. When we learn to accept rules given by our wiser elders, life will go on much smoother and many difficulties will be avoided. Bahá'u'lláh tells us that if we don't learn to listen to our parents, we won't learn to listen to His teachings. Obedience is something we need for our own development, hard though it can be!

When you learn to abide by rules, you will learn to carry them out even when no one is looking. You will be sensible when others are being stupid. You will learn to stand up for what is right, instead of being led into trouble by your peers. This will keep you safe and happy. How many things seem trivial in your life that are really for your own protection? For instance, your parents may ask you to wear a helmet and pads while you are riding on a bike or skateboard. They may ask you to come home at a certain time or ring them up if you are going to be late. When we love and honour our parents, we will want them to be happy too. Their wishes are for our well-being. How many rules can you think of which seem irritating but are really for your benefit? Can you write down some of them or talk about them?

There are many people who are rebels. Many of them choose to live life in a way that is different from the rest of society and make their own rules. Some take drugs or drop out of the system. Many make themselves unhappy and lonely and cut themselves off. If you need to question authority, can you do it respectfully? Can you learn the rules of your family, school and religion? Can you do what is right even when nobody is watching? Can you question a rule without moaning, whining, raging or getting into conflict? When you grow up, would you like your children to respect you? Do you have the courage to say sorry when your are wrong and to start again?

Here is a lovely quote from 'Abdu'l-Bahá:

> *"Comfort thy mother and endeavor to do what is conducive to the happiness of her heart."*[45]

It takes real maturity and love to do this. We only live with our parents for a short period of our lives and they give us the opportunity to learn so many good things we wouldn't learn without them.

Not long ago I visited a house which was next door to the house where I grew up. The lady living there happened to mention that they had a terrible problem with mice. Over thirty years ago I had secretly bred mice in the house next door along with my best friend who lived there. Both our parents were against this because they said we were encouraging wild mice in the area. So, secretly we continued to breed them in the shed. Before we knew it, our few mice had bred and bred and soon we had over sixty. Then one night, they made a hole in the side of the cage and they all escaped! The neighbourhood was soon overrun with mice and we children knew that we were responsible. Therefore, when so many years later I heard that there was still this mice problem, I couldn't help wondering if they were the descendants of our mice! I still feel uncomfortable about the consequences of that act of disobedience, even though at the time it seemed trivial to us.

Please ponder on the following quote of 'Abdu'l-Bahá:

"When in perfect obedience thou followest the path of the evident Light, thou mayest rest assured that in a little while life will find the Beloved, the seeker the Desired One and the traveller the Goal." [46]

Turn War into Peace

"The body of the human world is sick. Its remedy and healing will be the oneness of the kingdom of humanity. Its life is the Most Great Peace. Its illumination and quickening is love. Its happiness is the attainment of spiritual perfections."[47]

Today we are growing up with war all around us. Every day the news is full of atrocities. We see death in front of us on the television screen. We see our own soldiers flying off to war and being heralded as heroes. Planes practise flying low over our homes. Fashion is often camouflaged clothes which are inspired by war. Many of the most successful films are based on violence, death and killing. Toys for boys largely consist of weapons and lasers modelled on weapons of destruction. Martial arts have become very popular too, as in this society we are encouraged to learn self-defence because of the high crime rates in cities. From a very young age our minds are filled with the thought of war. Our heroes are modelled on the biggest and the toughest. Kindness and thoughtfulness for each other come very low on the list.

In the book '*Paris Talks*', 'Abdu'l-Bahá speaks of his sadness about war. He talks about a battle that happened many years ago, but he would still feel the same about all the wars that are happening now in the world. He tells us how he wonders—

> "*at the human savagery that still exists in the world! How is it possible for men to fight from morning until evening, killing each other, shedding the blood of their fellow-men: And for what object? To gain possession of a part of the earth! Even the animals, when they fight, have an immediate and more reasonable cause for their attacks! How terrible it is that men, who are of the higher kingdom, can descend to slaying and bringing misery to their fellow-beings, for the possession of a tract of land.*"[48]

'Abdu'l-Bahá goes on to talk about obtaining land and extending territory peaceably. He tells us that war is made for the satisfaction of men's ambitions; for the sake of wordly gain for the few, and how terrible misery is brought to numerous homes, breaking the hearts of hundreds of men and women and children. 'Abdu'l-Bahá continues,

> "*How many widows mourn their husbands, how many stories of savage cruelty do we hear! How many little orphaned children are crying for their dead fathers, how many women are weeping for their slain sons! There is nothing so heart-breaking and terrible as an outburst of human savagery!*"[49]

Then He charges all of us individually to concentrate

all the thoughts of our hearts on love and unity.

> *I charge you all that each one of you concentrate all the thoughts of your heart on love and unity....* "*When a thought of war comes, oppose it by a stronger thought of peace. A thought of hatred must be destroyed by a more powerful thought of love. Thoughts of war bring destruction to all harmony, well-being, restfulness and content.*
>
> *Thoughts of love are constructive of brotherhood, peace, friendship, and happiness.*" [50]

'Abdu'l-Bahá tells us that if we desire with all our heart for friendship with every race on earth, as the Bahá'í teachings tell us, our thoughts, spiritual and positive will spread and will become the desire of others, growing stronger and stronger until they reach the minds of all men. He tells us not to despair, to take heart and to show love to all because *"Love is the breath of the Holy Spirit in the heart of man."* [51] He tells us to take courage because God never forsakes His children who strive, work and pray. He tells us to have courage and if our hearts are filled with the desire for tranquillity and harmony, these thoughts will have an effect on the warring world. This will eventually bring success and universal brotherhood to the world.

We as children have been enormously blessed to have been brought up to understand that it is God's purpose for the unity of mankind to prevail on earth, and that mankind is one, whatever their race, colour or religion or creed may be. Our individual talents and gifts can be used, however young we are, for helping to bring about this peace on earth. Our lives will always have great meaning, when we learn to love and know God through His teachings. We are told that one soul can catch a country alight spiritually. What a destiny we all can have!

Mother Teresa, who was a wonderful nun, devoted her whole life to teaching and then caring for the poor in India and in different places of the world. She once tried to help a home of mentally handicapped children in Lebanon. They were stuck in the middle of fighting, without food.

Mother Teresa went to the Ambassador to ask him to stop the fighting. He replied that as much as he would like to do this it was impossible, even for a Saint. She replied that she and her sisters would pray for a miracle for the fighting to stop. He then promised that if this miracle happened, he would personally escort her to collect the children. He thought she was a little mad. The following day was a Holy day in the Catholic church. Mother Teresa prayed for a miracle and the next day, for no obvious reason, a cease fire was temporarily declared and Mother Teresa was safely escorted by the Ambassador to collect the children. They were all brought out without harm to a place of safety. This is a lovely example of prayer moving mountains.

Peace begins in our hearts and in our homes and with our friends and relations, and then it reaches out to the whole country, and then to other countries and to the whole world.

You could reflect on this quote of Bahá'u'lláh:

"Glory not in love for your country, but in love for all mankind."[52]

True Beauty

"Make Thy Beauty to be my food, and Thy presence my drink, and Thy pleasure my hope, and praise of Thee my action, and remembrance of Thee my companion, and the power of Thy sovereignty my succorer, and Thy habitation my home, and my dwelling-place the seat Thou hast sanctified from the limitations imposed upon them who are shut out as by a veil from Thee." [53]

Today physical beauty has become an important factor. Every magazine for young people is revered by society. The shops are full of beauty products and magazines are filled with top models. Photographers touch up the photos in these magazines to make them look perfect. The models often appear flawless and the photos are setting a very unrealistic model of beauty. Young people are striving to look like them in their bodies, hair, clothes and finding it impossible to achieve. This is ultimately leading to many psychological illnesses, especially among girls, because they feel they can never be beautiful enough. They are learning and getting convinced that outer beauty is everything. With these impossible and artificial standards they are becoming really discouraged about themselves and starting to dislike the shape of their own bodies.

What they don't yet understand is that outer beauty

is by no means everything; that physical beauty is temporary and just skin-deep. In fact, in some cases it is a disadvantage, because beautiful persons can never be sure if they are loved for their physical beauty or their personality. Physical beauty cannot last and as the beautiful models or persons get older, they may find themselves discarded. Sometimes a person can rely on his or her beauty and forget to acquire virtues and a loving kind personality. Do you know anyone who is beautiful but not kind?

True beauty is that which touches people's hearts far more than physical beauty. True and real beauty is inner beauty. This is the beauty that shines out from inside a person. This is the beauty that illuminates a person's eyes and face when they share their happiness and love with others. Think of your friends. Do you agree that the friends that really attract us are the warm, glowing, kind and friendly ones? Perhaps they laugh and spread happiness a lot. Probably they have a loving way that makes you feel wanted and good about yourself. Do you love these friends because of the shape of their legs or their body? No, when we really like or love someone we feel and see their qualities. There is nothing more beautiful than a warm radiant smile. It is like a light being switched on.

Here are two quotes from the Writings of 'Abdu'l-Bahá. You may like to write them down or memorise them.

...become so luminous that all your thoughts, words and actions will shine with the Spiritual Radiance dominating your soul,...[54]

True Beauty

Presentation Skill

Nothing illuminates a man's heart save the radiance which shines forth from the Kingdom of God![55]

It does not matter whether you are a baby or a hundred years old. Radiance will illuminate you. Joy and spiritual radiance is actually a tangible energy that radiates from your inner self. It can be seen and felt and it lifts the energy of those around you and makes them happy too. 'Abdu'l-Baha goes on to tell us that the happiness of man is in the fragrance of the love of God. Love of God within makes a person acquire his true or inner beauty.

I remember my friend Lizbeth telling me a story about her 13-year-old grandchild. This child was going to be a bridesmaid at a wedding. She was very shy and was very afraid to be a bridesmaid because she thought she was overweight and not as elegant as the other bridesmaids. Then Lizbeth gave her grandchild some loving advice that changed her life for the better. Lizbeth told the child to be herself. Lizbeth mentioned to the child that she might not be the most beautiful of all the girls but she could be the most radiant! And guess what happened. The bridesmaid that everybody remembered and noticed was Lizbeth's grandchild. From that day she tried to acquire good qualities and showed her inner beauty. She became a wonderful person.

Next time you are in a group of people, look around you. Which person do you notice the most? The ones who are smiling and cheerful and radiantly glad to be with their friends or the most beautiful one who may be making no effort to be joyous? If you are physically beautiful, you may feel that you don't need to make others happy. On the other hand, if you have inner beauty, your love will shine out and radiate happiness among others. I lovingly suggest that you all try to acquire the inner beauty, which is permanent and everlasting. Can you all work to be loving and radiant?

Here are some affirmations for you to practise, and as you know practice makes a person perfect.

- I am loveable as myself.
- I am radiant.
- I will love everybody.
- I will share happiness with all.
- I will try to acquire inner beauty.

Remind yourself that you are a very loveable being and who you were created to be by the Almighty God.

Presentation Skill

"...school children, from their earliest years, should learn to deliver speeches of high quality, so that in their leisure time they will engage in giving cogent and effective talks, expressing themselves with clarity and eloquence." [56]

You may think this is a very hard thing to do, but I can assure you that with simple practice, using a few tips, everyone can learn to deliver speeches. Even those of you who have reached the age of five can start to learn. You can learn how to stand and how to say a poem by heart with open and expressive faces. Then you can learn to give short talks about your pets or anything that is important to you. You can also learn to put together your ideas first and then write a few words on a small card just to prompt yourselves. Soon you will become so keen that you will want to do more and more. You can also learn to read aloud, using the punctuation to give yourselves plenty of expression.

As children, you will get a lot of opportunities to say prayers at festivals and other gatherings and meetings. You may simply read the prayers or say them by heart. Saying something by heart means to me more than saying it from memory; it means saying it from your heart as if you really mean the words. When you do this, you can inspire all around you by touching them with the words of the Holy Writings. The prayers and Writings have a spiritual language and there is nothing sadder than to hear them rushed and gabbled with no meaning coming across. These words are holy. They are a gift to us. They have the power to change us and heal us, and to help us grow if we allow them to. It is really important that we understand this.

Here are some simple tips to help you read and recite the Writings effectively. If you learn to do this, you will become a channel for Baha'u'llah's words to reach people. By saying prayers, you are speaking the language of heaven. First, you need to read the passage through and check that you can read the words and pronounce them properly. There will be many words that are new because the vocabulary is advanced. These difficult words will enrich your vocabulary in a way that you cannot imagine and your reading skills will become advanced. You can take the help of adults to assist you. If you don't say a prayer properly, it becomes a reading lesson in public, which defeats the purpose of prayer. Once prepared, please remember to read slowly and loud enough for other people in the room to hear. Every word is important, and try not to swallow the ends of the words. If you are brave and assured after a lot of practice, perhaps, you can look up at your audience briefly, remembering to keep a finger on the place where you are, to stop you losing your place.

Expression is very important. To read in an expressive way, we need to be guided by the punctuation. A comma means a pause. A full stop means a longer pause, because after a full stop the subject is changing.

I usually suggest pausing for the count of one or two for a full stop. An exclamation mark is used to show excitement or surprise, so you need to use your voice to show this. Can you practise saying, 'Oh no!', 'Help!', 'Oh bother!' Practice makes your voice sound surprised or worried. Then you need to look at question marks. Your voice goes up at the end when you ask a question. A lively expressive face makes all the difference. If you show the words in your face, your voice will reflect it too. If you are reading a poem, you need to find the key words that are really important and then you can say them with force. If you are pronouncing words like *soft, loud* or *hard*, you can practise softening or hardening your voice. It is the same with sounds. For instance, *'bang!'* would sound loud, and with *'zoom'* you would put emphasis on the letter *z*.

When you get to the last line, it is important not to drop your voice. If you do, anyone listening gets the sense that you are thinking 'thank goodness it's all over'. Try to make every word important, right up to the last one. Then pause and look up before rushing away. If you are standing, it is a good idea to have your feet apart and one foot slightly in front of the other. This stops you rocking or overbalancing. If you are holding a book, hold it at the heart level. If you cover your face, it stops you projecting the sound, as it goes into the book. If you hold the book too low, you will be looking down and your voice will be lost to the floor. This probably sounds a lot of instructions; but if you try some of these out with an adult, starting with a very easy picture book with few words, you will be surprised how quickly you learn to read or speak in front of an audience beautifully. These skills you will have all your life. Then you can teach them to your families and friends.

Perhaps you would like to start with a small poem. Read or say it out loud to your family. I am sure many of you with practice can become excellent readers and speakers and give a lot of pleasure to others.

References

1. *Hidden Words of Bahá'u'lláh* (Arabic), no. 59, Bahá'í Publishing Trust, New Delhi, India.
2. 'Abdu'l-Bahá, *Paris Talks*, p.122, Bahá'í Publishing Trust, New Delhi, India.
3. *Remembrance of God*, (Short Obligatory Prayer), p. 133, Bahá'í Publishing Trust, New Delhi, India.
4. *Hidden Words of Bahá'u'lláh* (Arabic), no. 11, Bahá'í Publishing Trust, New Delhi, India.
5. 'Abdu'l-Bahá, *Remembrance of God*, p. 95, Bahá'í Publishing Trust, New Delhi, India.
6. *Gleanings from the Writings of Bahá'u'lláh*, p. 260, Bahá'í Publishing Trust, New Delhi, India.
7. *The Compilation of Compilations*, p. 2. vol. 1, Bahá'í Publications Australia, 1991.
8. *Hidden Words of Bahá'u'lláh* (Arabic), no. 22, Bahá'í Publishing Trust, New Delhi, India.
9. *Lights of Guidance*, p.137, #457, Bahá'í Publishing Trust, New Delhi, India.
10. *The Compilation of Compilations*, p. 2. vol. 1, Bahá'í Publications Australia, 1991.
11. Bahá'u'lláh, *Prayers and Meditation*, p. 248, Bahá'í Publishing Committee, New York, USA.
12. *Tablets of Bahá'u'lláh*, p. 142, Bahá'í World Centre, Haifa.
13. 'Abdu'l-Bahá, *Bahá'í Prayers*, p. 72, Bahá'í Publishing Trust, Wilmette, Illinois, USA.
14. The author of this verse is not known.
15. 'Abdu'l-Bahá, *The Promulgation of Universal Peace*, p. 99, Bahá'í Publishing Trust, Wilmette, Illinois, USA.
16. *Hidden Words of Bahá'u'lláh* (Arabic), no. 4, Bahá'í Publishing Trust, New Delhi, India.

17. 'Abdu'l-Bahá, *Letter to Martha Root*.

18. *Hidden Words of Bahá'u'lláh* (Persian), no. 21, Bahá'í Publishing Trust, New Delhi, India.

19. Proverbs 3:5, *King James Bible*.

20. Psalm 27:1, *King James Bible*.

21. Luke 4:10, *King James Bible*.

22. 'Abdu'l-Bahá, *Paris Talks*, p. 29, Bahá'í Publishing Trust, New Delhi, India.

23. Luke 27:1, *King James Bible*.

24. 'Abdu'l-Bahá, *Paris Talks*, p. 61, Bahá'í Publishing Trust, New Delhi, India.

25. *Hidden Words of Bahá'u'lláh* (Arabic), no. 8, Bahá'í Publishing Trust, New Delhi, India.

26. *Selections from the Writings of 'Abdu'l-Bahá*, p. 179, Bahá'í World Centre, Haifa.

27. 'Abdu'l-Bahá, *Remembrance of God*, p. 95, Bahá'í Publishing Trust, New Delhi, India.

28. *Tablets of Bahá'u'lláh*, p. 264, Bahá'í World Centre, Haifa.

29. Bahá'u'lláh, *Kitáb-i-Iqan*, p. 195, Bahá'í Publishing Trust, New Delhi, India.

30. 'Abdu'l-Bahá, *The Promulgation of Universal Peace*, p. 453, Bahá'í Publishing Trust, Wilmette, Illinois, USA.

31. 'Abdu'l-Bahá, *Paris Talks*, p. 98, Bahá'í Publishing Trust, New Delhi, India.

32. Shoghi Effendi, *The Unfolding Destiny of the British Bahá'í Community*, p. 107, Bahá'í Publishing Trust, London, UK.

33. Shoghi Effendi, *Dawn of a New Day*, p. 36, Bahá'í Publishing Trust, New Delhi, India.

34. *Selections from the Writings of 'Abdu'l-Bahá*, p.130, Bahá'í World Centre, Haifa.

35. *Selections from the Writings of 'Abdu'l-Bahá*, p.132, Bahá'í World Centre, Haifa.

36. *Remembrance of God*, p. 6, no. 7, Bahá'í Publishing Trust, New Delhi, India.

37. *The Compilation of Compilations*, vol. I, p. 3910, Bahá'í Publications Australia, 1991.

38. 'Abdu'l-Bahá, *The Promulgation of Universal Peace*, p.185, Bahá'í Publishing Trust, Wilmette, Illinois, USA.

39. 'Abdu'l-Bahá, *Paris Talks*, p. 109, Bahá'í Publishing Trust, New Delhi, India.

40. *Compilation, Bahá'í Scriptures,* p. 450.

41. *Ridván Messages of the Universal House of Justice,* Ridván 155, 1998, p. 3.

42. *Reciting the Verses of God*, p. 228, Bahá'í Publishing Trust, New Delhi, India.

43. *Tablets of Bahá'u'lláh*, p. 155, Bahá'í World Centre, Haifa.

44. *The Compilation of Compilations,* vol. I, p. 387, Bahá'í Publications Australia, 1991.

45. 'Abdu'l-Bahá, *Bahá'í World Faith*, p. 361, Bahá'í Publishing Trust, Wilmette, Illinois, USA.

46. *Tablets of 'Abdu'l-Bahá*, vol. 3, p. 689.

47. 'Abdu'l-Bahá, *The Promulgation of Universal Peace*, p.19, Bahá'í Publishing Trust, Wilmette, Illinois, USA.

48. 'Abdu'l-Bahá, *Paris Talks*, p. 28, Bahá'í Publishing Trust, New Delhi, India.

49. 'Abdu'l-Bahá, *Paris Talks*, p. 29, Bahá'í Publishing Trust, New Delhi, India.

50. 'Abdu'l-Bahá, *Paris Talks*, p. 29, Bahá'í Publishing Trust, New Delhi, India.

51. 'Abdu'l-Bahá, *Paris Talks*, p. 30, Bahá'í Publishing Trust, New Delhi, India.

52. *Tablets of Bahá'u'lláh*, p. 138, Bahá'í Publications Australia, 1991.

53. Bahá'u'lláh, *Prayers and Meditation*, p. 261, Bahá'í Publishing Committee, New York, USA.

54. 'Abdu'l-Bahá, *Paris Talks*, p. 74, Bahá'í Publishing Trust, New Delhi, India.

55. 'Abdu'l-Bahá, *Tablets of 'Abdu'l-Bahá*, v.1, p. 53, Bahá'í Publishing Committee, New York, USA.

56. 'Abdu'l-Bahá, *Selections from the Writings of 'Abdu'l-Bahá*, p. 134, Bahá'í World Centre, Haifa.

Glossary

affirmation	a statement of truth
agony	sharp physical or mental pain
antidote	anything that relieves a harmful effect
apathy	lack of interest
apparent	clear
athlete	a person who is good in sports
atrocity	wicked or cruel act
bridesmaid	a girl or woman who accompanies a bride on her wedding day
brownie	a small square nutty chocolate cake
camouflage	a plan or disguise meant to cheat
capacity	the ability or power to do something
channel	a medium for communication
chaotic	in complete confusion or disorder
cherish	to feel or show kindness or care for
child minder	a person who looks after children
cogent	clear, logical, and convincing.
commandment	a command of God
communion	spiritual union
compassion	sympathy and concern for the sufferings of others
consolation	comfort received by someone after a loss or disappointment
contemplate	to think with continued attention
contentment	a state of peaceful happiness or satisfaction
conversation	exchange of information and ideas through speech
counsel	advice or guidance
courteous	polite and considerate in manner
curb	to control
depressed	sad; discouraged
destiny	fate; fortune

devoid (of)	entirely lacking or free from
dispel	to drive away
distinction	prominence; fame
distinguish	to separate from others by comparing
eloquence	effective language
embarrassment	the state of feeling awkward
embodiment	giving a visible form or body
enhance	to increase or improve
essence	the quality which determines the character of something
exhortation	a speech or written passage intended to persuade, inspire, or encourage
forsake	give up
foundation	that on which something is built; basis
frantic	fast in a wild and uncontrolled way
glade	an open space in a forest
God-centred	focused in God
harmony	agreement in action, opinion or feeling
harsh	severe or cruel
herald	to announce publicly
hinder	to block the progress
humankind	the human race; humanity
immune system	the various cells and tissues in the body to fight infection
indicator	something that shows or points out; sign
inestimable	not able to be measured
infectious	tending to spread from one person to another
material world	the world concerned with physical rather than spiritual interests.
meditate	to think upon; to reflect
mentally	in the mind
noble	of high moral qualities
nurture	to feed or support
obstacle	a person or thing that opposes or prevents
opportunity	a chance
organic	relating to or derived from living matter
overbalance	to lose or cause to lose balance

panic	a sudden uncontrollable feeling of fear or anxiety
peer	a person who is an equal in social standing, rank, or age
physically	in the body
ponder	consider carefully
potential	hidden but unrealized ability or capacity
prune	trim (a tree, shrub, or bush) by cutting away dead or overgrown branches or stems.
punctuation	the marks, such as full stop, comma, and brackets, used in writing to separate sentences and their elements and to clarify meaning.
radiant	bright; shining radiate to emit; to give out
rake	to gather or remove by a rake (a hand tool)
rebel	one who refuses to obey an authority
reed	a piece of thin cane or metal which vibrates in a current of air to produce the sound of various musical instruments
reflect	think
relative [adj.]	having meaning only in relation to something else
reveal	disclose; uncover
slump	to slip down, to bend
sovereignty	supreme power or authority
spiritual	relating to the spirit or soul and not to physical nature or matter
stifle	to suppress
strive	to try hard
succour	help or assistance in times of difficulty and distress
surgeon	a medical practitioner who specialises in surgery
talent	a natural ability or skill
tangible	clear and definite
tend	to look after
terminal illness	a disease ending in death
territory	an area under the jurisdiction of a ruler or state
texture	the surface of a material
thanksgiving	an expression of thanks to God
tranquillity	silence and calm

transform	to change
unique	being the only one of a particular type; without equal or like
uplifting	raise morally or spiritually
vicinity	a surrounding, adjacent, or nearby area; neighbourhood
vocabulary	the group of words known to an individual person
volunteer	a person who freely offers to do something
weapons of destruction	weapons that cause heavy damage to life and property
whisper	speak very softly
woodland	a land that is mostly covered with woods or dense growths of trees and shrubs